Thailand Travel Tips and Advice

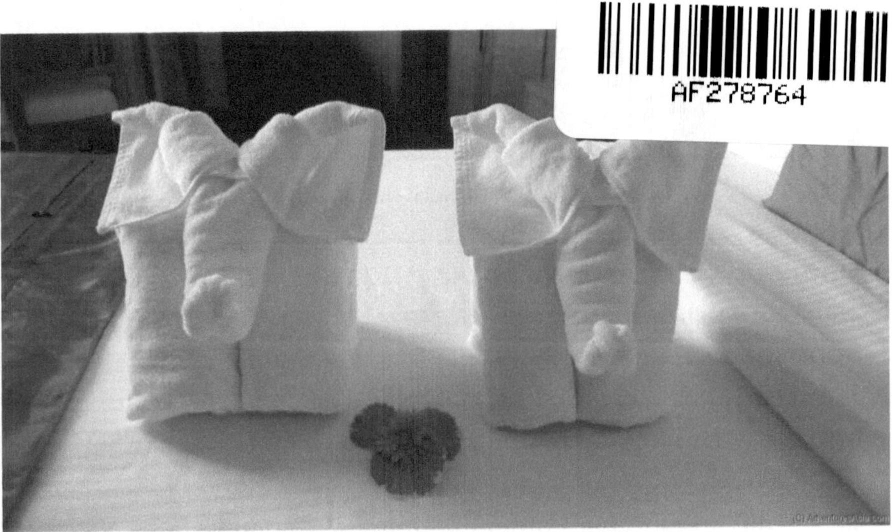

Heading to Thailand for the first time? Congratulations! Thailand is such a wonderful country ... So much so I live here Here is my tips page that is just jammed packed with Thailand Travel Tips and Advice. With so many flights to and from the Kingdom, here are the most important tips I would like to share:

Contents

Accommodation

Thailand has many levels of accommodation with lodgings to suit any budget. Main tourist areas cater for the budget conscious traveler with basic fan rooms to exclusive 5-star palatial retreats.

Breakfasts:

Most three-star plus hotels include a Western/Asian buffet breakfast in the room charge. The food quality can vary and if your hotel does not include breakfast or you feel like a change, look for cheap restaurants around most hotels for alternative options. A toasted ham and cheese sandwich from 7-11 does the job for me if in a pinch.

Internet Access:

Most hotels offer in house internet Wifi. Quality of signal can vary depending on room and resort location. On Smaller Islands like Koh Phi-Phi (near Phuket) or Koh Tao (near Koh Samui) you can expect slow connections with the mainland. It is recommended to get a 4G data/phone sim card from 7-11 as the 4G data connection is very good from all main networks (DTAC, True, AIS etc.) even on most islands. Passport is required for a new sim card in Thailand.

Room Rates:

Pricing is usually a quarter to a half of what you would pay for similar lodgings in western-based countries. I recommend air conditioning as a must and is usually always included.

Food Room Service:

Usually good value in price and quality. Room service also usually attracts a 10% service charge and a VAT Tax of 7%. Most menus include Asian, Western and European selections.

Power Supply:

Voltage is 220 volts via 2 flat pins. It is recommended to get the pin converter before you leave to allow you use your own appliance/devices. Airport Duty-Free is a good place to pick up the right one (tax-free after you clear immigration). For example, your battery chargers, hair dryers, and notebook computers may require an adapter. If from the US, you will need a 110v to 240v transformer.

Safety Deposit Boxes:

Most hotels offer key based safety deposit boxes for free, usually at a separate desk at reception or in your room. I would recommend you keep your credit cards, flight tickets, passport, and extra cash in there. I have had no problem with theft, but it is best to be safe so as not to spoil your travels.

Sleeping:

The best thing after hard days sightseeing is good sleep. Since Thailand is always on the go, places like Bangkok, Patong Beach (Phuket) and Pattaya can always be noisy from the traffic, discotheques, car horns, hotel entertainment and intoxicated tourists in your hotel.

So go to the chemist/drug store before you leave and grab yourself a pack of small foam earplugs. Not only will they give you great sleep in your hotel but also on your plane flights. Eyeshades also are a great sleeping aid if you feel

like sleeping in after a big night out or on plane flights. I personally use noise-canceling headphones while traveling, currently Bose QC II's.

Alcohol

Arriving in Thailand, your duty-free liquor limit is 1 liter (1.125 Liter is fine).

Alcohol is available everywhere in Thailand. Convenience stores like 7 Eleven, Big C, Tesco Lotus are the biggest suppliers to the tourist market. Specialist liquor shops can also be found. A law came into effect late 2005 whereby one can now only purchase alcohol from the hours of 11 am to 2 pm and 5 pm to 12 am.

It is customary to give a small tip to the waitress when paying for a drink. Most of the times they will give you back change including many small Baht coins implied for the tip.

The local Thai whiskey which is very strong is called 'Samsom'. Their rum is called 'Hong Thong'. It is normally mixed with soda water and is very cheap to buy.

Backpackers

Thailand is very suited to backpackers. It is hot, cheap and a friendly nation of people.

Backpackers obviously should pack at least as possible. Wear cotton underwear and shirts if possible. Sandals are ideal for comfortable walking. Think about buying new cheap tee shirts/dresses while traveling around in Thailand which could be just as cheap and as washing your old one.

Make sure you also pack a key lock and a small torch.

In Bangkok, most international backpackers hang out and meet up at Khao San Road (see photo below). Expect to find food hawkers, guest houses, nightclubs, hair beaders, clothes retailers, bars, souvenir sellers and travel agencies along the road. Quickest way there is by Tuk Tuk. Many of the cities major Temples and Palaces are also near Khao San Road.

In Chiang Mai old city you will find guesthouses galore in the small soi's (lanes). These guesthouses are essentially backpacker level accommodation.

JEEP TREK 4WD
THANA & PARADISE
TEL: 281-9786, 2839637
MOBILE: 01-6130564
PLACE TOUR
KKING
CHIANGMAI
PAI AREA
INFORMATION
PLEASE
Thai
MARCOPOLO
(C) AdventuresAsia.com

ADVENTURES ASIA
Around Asia Travel Blog

Climate

It is said that there are three seasons in Thailand:

* *Hot and Dry (Summer) – which is around March to June*

* *Warm and Rainy (Monsoonal)– which is around July to October*

* *Cool and Less Humid (Winter) – which is around November to February.*

Most of southern Thailand can be said to really only have 2 seasons – wet and a dry, with the temperature the same all year round.

In northern cities like Chiang Mai and Chiang Rai it can be quite cool at nights from November to February. The humidity is low and it is a great time to travel.

The humidity is the real scorcher in Thailand at around 70 – 80% all year. So expect to sweat in non-air-conditioned areas. Average temperatures range from 20 – 35 degrees Celsius.

Take extra singlets and underwear. Thongs or sandals are preferable. You can get into nightclubs in shorts and sandals/thongs if a tourist, so dress for comfort is the rule.

Make sure you take one rain jacket for rainy days and a jumper for the flight to and from Thailand. I am sure the cabin temperature on board planes these days is around 16 degrees Celsius. Blooding freezing.

Clothing

Thailand travel tips for packing:

Before I recommend what you should pack, the following list could be your initial shopping adventure for Thailand as all these items are available at very cheap prices.

It is recommended to pack:

* *Cotton shirts*
* *Cotton shorts*
* *Cotton trousers*
* *Cotton underwear*
* *Hat*
* *Swimming costumes*
* *Sarong*
* *Sandals*
* *Sunscreen*
* *Sunglasses*
* *Thongs/Flip flops*

The biggest national Shopping Center chain is called 'Big C'. You will find all that there.

When visiting some Temples you will be expected to cover your shoulders and knees for religious reasons. You must also wear closed footwear with sandals being acceptable. Covering your shoulders and knees are usually required for the most important Temples; such as the First Class Royal Temples eg. <u>The Grand Palace</u> in Bangkok.

Tailors are also in abundance in Thailand and will within 24 hours copy your favorite garment, create any shorts, trousers, suits, dresses etc. The special deal price is usually US$199 for 3 full suits tailor made.

Many Tailors are situated within Hotel Complexes for your convenience. For men, the suit package is usually a summer suit, 2 business suits plus 2 silk ties, 2 leather belts and maybe even a Silk Kimono could be thrown in. For women, the deal is usually for 2 business suits, a summer suit, 2 blouses, 1 dress, 1 silk scarf and a bonus like a kimono. Great Value you would have to agree...

Customs

Arriving in Thailand

Make sure you fill in the white arrivals passenger card of which you will only receive on the plane. I always do this at the airport before I leave as I have many spare cards on hand. This leads me to recommend that you get to the passport control line as soon as possible as it is possible to wait in line for 30 minutes to an hour to get processed if it is at night and other flights have also just arrived. Baggage collection can also be a slow process.

Departing Bangkok

Expect delays at passport control when leaving during the day time. I like doing immigration at another airport to save time in Bangkok eg. Chiang Mai International Airport where immigration is always under five minutes.

Do not purchase fake weapons in Thailand. If you purchase any swords do make sure you pack them in your main luggage and not in your carry on luggage.

You also must have export licenses for Antiques and images of Buddha. It is said that you can expect bad luck (bad karma) if you take any artifacts away from Thailand.

Food

Thai cuisine has to be one of the main reasons to travel to Thailand. From cheap hand pushed mobile street vendors to exclusive restaurants, Thailand has it all.

Available in abundance are local fruits, seafood, meats like chicken, pork and beef, sweets, pastries and even cooked insects (that's right).

The local seafood available is amazing as it is fresh daily. Many restaurants have a seafood selection buffet on ice out the front of their restaurants.

A walk along Patong Beach Road, Ao Nang Beach Road, Whitesands Beach Koh Chang, and Pattaya Beach Roads at night you will see a huge range of live seafood you can buy per 100 per grams.

Purchase treats like lobster, huge river prawns, fish, and mussels all cooked to the way you like it. In Phuket, you can buy the famous Phuket Lobster for about per 100 grams with the average lobster weighing around a kilo (1000 grams). In the main tourist areas, you will also find specific foods on offer like Indian, German, Japanese, Korean and Russian cuisines.

Expect to also see every fast food chain near the main tourist areas in Thailand. Usually not as good value as the local food and expensive when compared to Thai food, but can be a welcome home sick comfort meal.

I highly recommend the pork kebabs from the street food vendors. Extremely tasty, good value, and delicious after a night out sampling the local beers: Chang, Leo, and U-Beer.

Whole fruits like the small local pineapple are sweet and delicious. It can be peeled and cut up in a bag with a kabab skewer to eat it with.

To receive your food bill, just say "Check Bin". It is the same as "Check Please".

Try to give a small tip if you enjoyed your meal. 20 Baht is always appreciated.

We also recommend that you take diarrhea tablets from your home country just in case you get a tummy ache. Always better to be safe than sorry

Hygiene

For first time travelers to the "Land of Smiles', the pungent smells can easily overwhelm sensitive stomachs. This is most prevalent while walking the streets where the sewer system is just a few feet deep under the walking pavement on the sides of the road. They have small air holes in the cement pavement which can release an odor. Having a handkerchief close by is recommended.

It must be also noted that Thai's use the Asian squat-style toilet. Western-style hotels have western toilets but expect public toilets and toilets in service stations to be the Thai style. Take some travel tissues with you in your daily travel bag is a good tip.

When at nightclubs and some pubs, make sure you have small change available to tip the toilet attendant. Toilets in nightclubs are usually western style.

Vaccinations are recommended prior to visiting the Kingdom of Thailand. Please check with your local doctor.

Other hygiene tips include:

* *Do not drink or gargle the local water*
* *Buy only bottled water*
* *Take diarrhea pills with you*
* *Wash sweaty clothing regularly*

Insurance

Simply a Must have!

The old rule is "If you cannot afford travel insurance you cannot afford to travel".

Renting a Moped?

You must have a valid motorcycle license and an International Drivers Permit from your own country for travel insurance to cover you if involved in an accident.

If you have been robbed while in Thailand, ring the Travel Police on 1555. This is a national Thailand number. You must produce a local police report to be paid out by your insurance company when you get back home. After you ring the travel police, ring the insurance hotline number provided by your insurance company. When you pay for your travel insurance you will receive this emergency contact information.

Keep your important documents like monies and personal effects in the hotels' safety deposit box near reception or in the room safe.

Try also to keep a photocopy of your passport, air tickets, vouchers, insurance, atm cards in a separate location in case the originals get stolen. I like to have a copy in my main travel wallet and on my pc.

Jet Skis

It must be noted that most upscale hotels frown on promoting the use of Jet Skis. They often state this in their room information folder.

This is due to the noise, pollution, accidents and the possibility of no insurance being available.

You can rent a Jet Skis on Jomtien Beach pear Pattaya per hour. Patong Beach and the beaches of Koh Samui, Koh Samet and Koh Chang are a bit more expensive.

Language

When visiting a new country you always feel more comfortable when you know a few words of the local language.

Most shopkeepers speak good English. The hint here is to speak slowly so they can work out what you are saying. If you talk too fast they will stare at you and say 'slow, slow ...". If they cannot understand you they may say "yes, yes ...", so be careful.

Laundry

Due to the high humidity of Thailand, you will go through your clothes very quickly due to the continued sweating especially if out and about.

Hotel laundry prices are very cheap when compared to western standards and only takes 24 hours to complete.

We recommend that if you are at one place for a few days to seek out a street laundry service for the best value. They normally charge by kilo ironed or non-ironed.

Local Transport

There are many types of local city transport in Thailand. They are:

Songthaew

Usually, Songthaew's are long tray utes with seats down each side covered to protect passengers from the rain. They circle areas continually and the fare costs per person.

In Chiang Mai, there are a few different colors that the songthaews are painted. Each color represents a different area of the city they only service.

To get on a Songthaew, simply wait for them to honk their horn and then turn around and acknowledge them and they will stop for you, or wave your hand as they drive by. If

you are unsure of the usual fare for your destination, ask and confirm with the driver first.

To get off the Songthaew, press one of the buzzer buttons around the back of the vehicle. The maximum is around 12 passengers. If you have more than 5 people in your group feel free to negotiate a better group price.

Tuk Tuk

Tuk Tuk's are 3 wheeled two-stroke vehicles that can fit up to 3 passengers into the back, though I have seen up to 5 Thai's in the back. Tuk Tuk's are very noisy and the pollution is very bad in areas like Bangkok due to the high traffic levels. You may need to cover your mouth and nose with a handkerchief.

Tuk Tuk drivers nearly always have a second motive to get you in the vehicle in central Bangkok. They will push and push to get you to visit a gems dealer on the way to the location you were wanting to visit. If you do not wish to see the gem shop – where the gems are overvalued or fake – you must confirm this with the driver before you hop on. Many drivers will snub you sometimes if you do not go to the gem shops as they will not receive their kickback payments.

Motorcycle Taxi

Simply hop on the back without any helmet after you work out the fare. Prevalent in all areas of Thailand. You will see groups of young men with motorcycles on corners of streets. They have a uniform with a number and are licensed by the government. I do not recommend the use of this form of transport in Bangkok due to the traffic.

Car Taxi

Similar to the metered taxi's in western countries, though a lot cheaper. You will have the option of using the meter or paying a fixed priced. Meter is the best option as you are only charged for distance traveled as the traffic can be very slow.

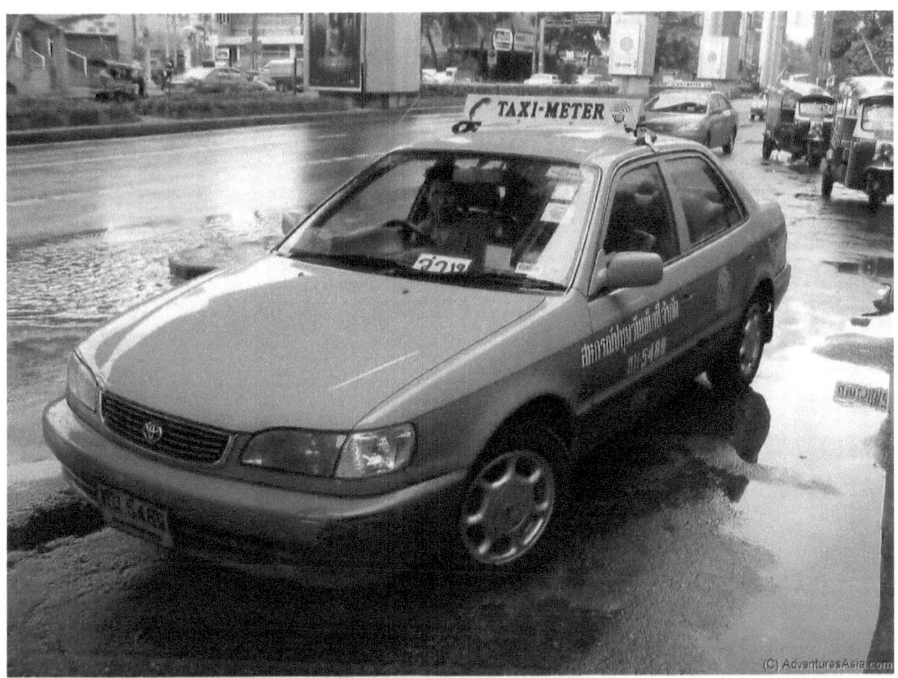

Sky Train

The Sky Train opened in 2000 and services the main areas of Bangkok. It is a quiet pollution free form of transport at a very cheap price. The advantage of this mode of transport is that it is air-conditioned, quick, safe and has stops to all main tourist areas like Patong Night Markets and Chatuchak Weekend Markets. The best form of transport in Bangkok!

MRT (Mass Rapid Transport)

An underground MRT System operates servicing other areas of Bangkok intersecting the two Sky Train Lines. The fee structure is similar to the Sky Train rates and the service which is identical to the Singapore MRT system is first class. Be sure to stop at Lumphini Station to visit the Suanlum Night Bazaar.

Vehicle Hire

There are also many hire car and bike options in all tourist areas. Make sure you have your International Drivers License permit before you travel to Thailand.

The best tip I can give is to make sure that the vehicle is insured before you hire it.

Local Buses

The cheapest way to travel around Thailand is by the local and domestic bus network. The network features both air-conditioned (VIP) services and non-air-conditioned services with the air-conditioned services costing slightly more. Most local Thai people use the bus network to get to and from destinations and are also a favored way to travel by budget-minded backpackers. Not for me though. Domestic air travel in Thailand is very affordable.

Massage

There are 2 main Thai Massages – Thai Oil and Traditional Thai. Costs vary depending on your location but on average the price is 200 Baht for per hour for Thai, 300 for Oil.

Hotel in-house rates are normally twice as expensive than street-based rates but can be done in your own hotel room.

If you visit a large massage parlor, you can choose from up to 30 or more trained girls in varying ages over 18. Ask the manager for recommendations of the best masseur for your treatment.

Traditional Thai massage is an amazing massage. You walk out feeling like a new person, ready for sightseeing or more

shopping. They stretch, pull and massage every muscle in your body (strictly no sex).

If you have had previous back surgery, make sure you inform the girl before the message starts to the location. They sometimes walk along your spine in the treatment process.

Thai oil massage is more the slow deep muscle massage using the soft base of coconut oil. It is very easy to fall asleep while receiving this massage.

Foot massages are also very popular as to are head and hand massages. These messages last from 1 to 2 hours and cost around 200 – 300 Baht per hour.

Nightlife

Thailand is world renown for its colorful nightlife!

Each of the main destinations in Thailand has their own nightlife area. The nightlife varies from drinking bars to discotheques and Go-Go bars.

The main spots are:

Bangkok *– Patpong Night Markets Area, Asoke (Soi Cowboy) and Nana Plaza.*

Chiang Mai *– Near the Night Markets is the Chiang Mai Entertainment Complex on Loi Kror Road.*

Hua Hin *– Between Damnern Kasem Road and Soi Kanjanomai.*

Koh Chang - The main bars are located at White Sand Beach along with the sole nightclub on the island.

Koh Samet - A few bars are dotted along the main west coast of the island.

Koh Samui - Chaweng, Lamai and Mae Nam Beaches.

Pattaya - Walking Street and Soi 1 - Soi Diamond.

Phuket - Bangla Road and Patong Beach Road.

All large tourist destinations will have some sort of local bars area.

Drinking Bars

Drink Prices can vary widely. All establishments usually have bar girls to chat with you. They make their income from you buying them 'Lady Drinks'. Bar girls talk to both men and women.

Many drinking bars have bar games to play with the girls like Connect Four, Jackpot, Dice games and a fun game where you have to drive a nail all the way into a tree stump in one go with a hammer. It is not very easy while under the effects of the local beers like Chang Beer.

Go-Go Bars

Formed in the early post wars days of the Vietnam War, Go-Go bars feature the latest music and scantily clad girls. Entry is free, but drink prices are maybe 20-40% higher than at normal drinking bars.

Along the Patpong Night Markets in Bangkok and Bangla Road in Patong Beach in Phuket, you will find touts on the sidewalks with cards listing acts in live sex shows at specific Go-Go bars. Again, entry is usually free or around 200 Baht including a free drink, but make sure you check

the list of acts to make sure you really do want to go in. Drink prices are similar to normal Go-Go bar prices.

Nightclubs and Discoteques

Most nightclubs feature the latest western and local Thai dance music mixed. Often throughout the night, stage shows will be performed singing western or Thai songs. Entry to the clubs costs around 200 Baht and usually includes a free drink. Drinks, as usual, are more expensive at nightclubs.

Parasailing

Parasailing is a big attraction in Pattaya, Koh Samui and in Phuket.

Locations like Jomtien Beach in Pattaya, along Chaweng Beach in Koh Samui and along Patong Beach in Phuket are most popular.

With a height of 150 – 200 meters in Thailand makes it very exciting but also more dangerous.

Many parasailing companies have now been forced to set up offshore pontoon structures to for customers to take-off from. This was due to the increasing amount of accidents near the shoreline. Each ride usually includes a quick rise into the air, slow drop into the water for a quick dunk, then another rise up, then the landing. Take care

when you take off and keep your legs up until you clear of the pontoon. Make sure you have travel insurance too!

Police

There are two types of Police in Thailand. The normal police and the Tourist Police.

Always contact the tourist police if you have any hassles like theft or drugs. You can ring them anywhere in Thailand on 1155.

Travel police can converse in English and are slighter better paid than regular police so not as likely to be bribed. You will see travel police locations in all the main tourist locations.

A word on drugs: Never ever accept anything from anyone! Most street cigarette sellers always sell illegal drugs like marijuana and amphetamines as well. If you do purchase a drug from them, you risk the seller turning you into the police for a quick reward.

If you do get caught with hard drugs, expect long jail terms and heavy fines.

Public Holidays

The main public holiday period in Thailand is Songkran or Thai New Year and occurs mid-April.

It must be noted that traffic in and out of Bangkok on Public Holiday periods is very congested due to the Bangkok residents going to the country provinces to see relatives.

January:
New Years Day (1st)

February:
Chinese New Year Day
Makha Bucha Day

April:
Chakri Day (6th)
Songkran Festival (13-15)

May:
National Labour Day (1st)
Coronation Day
Ploughing Ceremony Day
Wisakha Bucha Day

July:
Asarnha Bucha Day
Buddhist Lent Day

August:
H.M. The Queen's Birthday (12th) – *Mothers Day*

October:
Chulalongkorn Day (23rd)

December:
H.M. The King's Birthday (5th) – *Fathers Day*
Constitution Day (10th)
New Year Eve (31st)

Most 3.5 star hotels up will charge for Gala Dinners which are normally held on Christmas Eve and New Year's Eve.

This is compulsory and the cost can be quite expensive so make sure you confirm these details before confirming your accommodation.

Religion

Thailand is a Royal Kingdom. Never insult the King or Queen of Thailand. Thai people highly respect the Royal family. They even have public holidays for both the birth dates of the current King and Queen also known as Fathers Day and Mothers Day respectively.

Buddhism is the main religion in Thailand. You will see a Wat or Temple in every Ban or Village and a small shrine at every house and business complex.

When creating or upgrading local Buddhist temples, local residents often donate money to the Wat and in return give thanks to Buddha and have their name engraved in a tile or plaque for life.

There are of course many other religions in Thailand. Some have even created western style churches to reflect their faith.

Please make sure your knees and shoulders are covered when visiting a First Class Royal Temple. Sandals are the minimum accepted for footwear, and hats should be taken off when entering temples.

Thai people normally do not shake hands when they greet one another. Instead, they press their palms together in a prayer-like gesture called a "Wai" including a small head bow.

Thai people also regard the head as the highest part of the body, literally and figuratively. Therefore, please avoid touching people on the head. It is considered very rude, especially to children and statues of Buddha.

Also, make sure you remove your shoes before entering a private Thai home.

Shopping

Shopping is one of the main reasons to visit Thailand. Bargains are aplenty.

Available on the main streets of tourist areas like Bangkok, Hua Hin, Koh Chang, Koh Samet, Koh Samui, Phuket, Pattaya, and Chiang Mai are exciting bargains like:

* *Art*
* *Bags & Backpacks*
* *Designer Jeans*
* *Gems & Jewelry*
* *Handbags & Wallets*
* *Hats*
* *Lacquerware*
* *DVDs*
* *Oil Paintings*
* *Photo Albums*
* *Shell ware*
* *Socks*
* *Souvenirs*
* *Sunglasses*
* *Wooden Carvings*

Now a lot of commercial items you will see offered is fake or pirated. Everything has been copied for sale to tourists. It is a massive industry and most of Asia does it.

You should barter when shopping in Thailand. All shops except fixed price department stores expect you to barter. It sounds unbelievable but you should start around one-third of their asking price and work your way up. Most times you should be able to get the items at 50% off the asking price.

My tip is once you reach the maximum you want to pay, walk away stating the same maximum price on every comeback price. If they do not say "Yes, Yes, Okay …", you know you have reached the cost price or close to it. You may wish to consider paying more if you really want the product as they will not sell it less than cost price. Try also to smile while bartering, it is considered more polite and makes the whole process more fun.

If you are the first buyer of the day, you can expect a better than normal price due to the Thai's believing the first day's sale is good luck. You can expect to be delayed for a few minutes while they bless all their goods with the bank notes you paid. It's great to watch. When you buy and Gems, make sure the business is ISO 9002 government certified.

Songkran Festival – Thai New Year

Songkran is the Thailand New Year Water Festival. It heralds the start of the rainy or monsoon season and the Thai New Year. It occurs early April and takes place over a few days.

Locals and tourists get into the spirit by splashing water and water-based paint everywhere. They splash it in the streets, over people, in businesses, on cars, everywhere. It is truly crazy! Crazy fun.

The spraying of water to passersby is considered good luck as they are in fact blessing you.

Songkran dinner is compulsory at most hotels during this period. Please factor this extra cost into your budget and keep that night free.

This festival is a real party period for the locals. They will drink for days with no sleep which can attribute to many accidents. It is estimated that hundreds of people every year die in the Songkran festival. That is not a misprint. Most due to drinking driving related accidents. So please be careful on the roads if attending Songkran!

Facts about Thailand

* *Known as Siam until 1939*
* *It is the only Southeast Asian country never to have been taken over by a European power*
* *Ports and harbors are Bangkok, Laem Chabang, Pattani, Phuket, Sattahip, Si Racha, Songkhla*
* *Coastline is 3,219 km long*
* *The name "Thailand" means "Land of the Free"*
* *Doi Inthanon is Thailand's highest peak (near Chiang Mai)*
* *The Mekong River forms a border between Thailand and Laos*
* *Phuket is Thailand's largest island*
* *Thailand's largest reclining Buddha image can be found in the Bangkok temple 'Wat Po'*
* *Bangkok has a population of 8+ Million with a total of 69+ million nationally*
* *Land mass is just over 500,000 square kilometers*
* *Humidity is a constant high at 70 – 80% except in the North during winter*
* *Currency is the Thai Baht*
* *Religion is mainly Buddhism comprising 95% of the country*

Thailand has 76 provinces which are *Amnat Charoen, Ang Thong, Buriram, Chachoengsao, Chai Nat, Chaiyaphum, Chanthaburi, Chiang Mai, Chiang Rai, Chon Buri, Chumphon, Kalasin, Kamphaeng Phet, Kanchanaburi, Khon Kaen, Krabi, Krung Thep Mahanakhon (Bangkok), Lampang, Lamphun, Loei, Lop Buri, Mae Hong Son, Maha Sarakham, Mukdahan, Nakhon Nayok, Nakhon Pathom, Nakhon Phanom, Nakhon Ratchasima, Nakhon Sawan, Nakhon Si*

Thammarat, Nan, Narathiwat, Nong Bua Lamphu, Nong Khai, Nonthaburi, Pathum Thani, Pattani, Phangnga, Phatthalung, Phayao, Phetchabun, Phetchaburi, Phichit, Phitsanulok, Phra Nakhon Si Ayutthaya, Phrae, Phuket, Prachin Buri, Prachuap Khiri Khan, Ranong, Ratchaburi, Rayong, Roi Et, Sa Kaeo, Sakon Nakhon, Samut Prakan, Samut Sakhon, Samut Songkhram, Sara Buri, Satun, Sing Buri, Sisaket, Songkhla, Sukhothai, Suphan Buri, Surat Thani, Surin, Tak, Trang, Trat, Ubon Ratchathani, Udon Thani, Uthai Thani, Uttaradit, Yala, and Yasothon.

VAT Refund

When purchasing large items in Thailand like electrical products, you may qualify to receive a refund on your VAT – Value Added tax. This is the equivalent to GST/VAT/Sales Tax.

This makes the products the same as duty-free prices. Please note that items like gemstones cannot have the VAT component refunded.

A VAT Refund will only occur if the items purchased are removed from Thailand within 60 days of the purchase date. The items must be purchased from participating businesses that show the 'VAT Refund For Tourists' logo.

On any one day, the items purchased from an individual participating business must not be less than 2,000 Baht including the VAT plus the total amount claiming for the VAT Refund must not be less than 5,000 Baht including the VAT amount.

All International departure terminals have VAT Refund counters just after you complete immigration formalities.

Water

Please do not drink the tap water in Thailand.

Some places say the water is fine but the bottled water is very cheap and it is not worth the risk to your trip. Do not even the gargle the water for washing your teeth.

It is always recommended to have bottled water on hand due to the continued intense humidity of Thailands climate.

△ Back to TOP

www.ingramcontent.com/pod-product-compliance
Lightning Source LLC
Chambersburg PA
CBHW032132050726
47590CB00008B/3061